poems
for
life

CELEBRITIES CHOOSE
THEIR FAVORITE POEM *and*
SAY WHY IT INSPIRES THEM

Yo-Yo Ma ✦ Joyce Carol Oates ✦ Stephen Sondheim
Allen Ginsberg ✦ Angela Lansbury ✦ Kurt Vonnegut
Harolyn Blackwell ✦ Isabella Rossellini ✦ Bill Irwin
E. L. Doctorow ✦ David Mamet ✦ Elie Wiesel
Ally Sheedy ✦ *and many more*

Introduction by Anna Quindlen

Arcade Publishing ✦ New York

Arcade Publishing books may be purchased in bulk at special discounts for sales promotion, corporate gifts, fund-raising, or educational purposes. Special editions can also be created to specifications. For details, contact the Special Sales Department, Arcade Publishing, 307 West 36th Street, 11th Floor, New York, NY 10018 or info@skyhorsepublishing.com.

Arcade Publishing® is a registered trademark of Skyhorse Publishing, Inc.®, a Delaware corporation.

Visit our website at www.arcadepub.com.

10 9 8 7 6 5 4 3 2 1

Library of Congress Cataloging-in-Publication Data is available on file.

Designed by Jeff Ward
Cover design: Erin Seaward-Hiatt
Front cover images © John Schreiner / Getty Images (flowers); © Katsumi Murouchi / Getty Images (watercolor background)

ISBN: 978-1-950994-36-6
Ebook ISBN: 978-1-62872-276-5

Printed in the United States of America

Contents

Preface

The inspiration behind this project, which was begun in 1992, was an Irish poetry anthology called *Lifelines*. *Lifelines* consists of a collection of letters and poems sent in by well-known figures in Ireland at the request of a group of Dublin students. These students found a publisher for the book, which they dedicated to the "children of the Third World," then donated all their royalties to organizations that might assist these children.

Our thought was to do something in the same spirit and to the same purpose. At Nightingale-Bamford, poetry is an integral part of the fifth-grade curriculum. In addition to writing their own poems, the students read and memorize a variety of poetry during the year, culminating in a recitation for their parents. Moreover, when students enter the middle school, they become involved in class projects dealing with social service. It therefore seemed very fitting to combine the fifth-grade social-service project with part of their English curriculum. We wanted the students not only to be awakened to a world of poetry through other people's choices, but to become aware of a world of need outside their immediate communities, one to which they could in some way contribute. We decided the proceeds of our project should benefit the International Rescue Committee, and more specifically the Women's Commission for Refugee Women and Children (a division of the IRC). The students were already familiar with this particular organization because Mary Anne Schwalbe, staff director, had come to the school and talked about her experiences with refugee women and children on several occasions.

For two years, the students wrote to well-known people in all fields. Every day, they awaited the mail with eager anticipation. When a reply arrived it was greeted with curiosity and excitement. Each letter and accompanying poem was read in class, and the poem and poet discussed. We greatly enjoyed finding out why people had selected a particular work, and we learned from what they had to say about it. What most struck all of us was how important poetry had been in the lives of the contributors, who had turned and returned to poems for amusement, solace, wisdom, and, perhaps most importantly, to find some part of themselves.

We are extremely grateful to all those who took the time to send in their thoughts and poems. We would also like to thank Timothy Bent, our editor at Arcade, who had such faith in the project; Mary Anne Schwalbe of the International Rescue Committee; The Nightingale-Bamford School teachers and administrators; and, most of all, the students of Class V from 1993 and 1994, whose names appear at the end of the volume.

Faith O'Grady
Mary Allen

Introduction
"Poetry Emotion"
by Anna Quindlen

Yusef Komunyakaa won the Pulitzer Prize, but he does not expect to become a household name, and not because his name itself, phonetically simple once parsed out bit by bit, looks at first glance so unpronounceable. Mr. Komunyakaa won the prize for poetry in a world that thinks of Pound and Whitman as a weight and a sampler, not an Ezra, a Walt, a thing of beauty, a joy forever.

It's hard to figure out why this should be true, why poetry has been shunted onto a siding at a time, a place, so in need of brevity and truth. We still use the word as a synonym for a kind of lovely perfection, for an inspired figure skater, an accomplished ballet dancer. Many of the finest books children read when young are poetry: *The Cat in the Hat, Goodnight Moon,* the free verse of *Where the Wild Things Are.*

And then suddenly, just as their faces lose the soft curves of babyhood, the children harden into prose and leave verse behind, or reject it entirely. Their summer reading lists rarely include poetry, only stories, "The Red Badge of Courage," not Mr. Komunyakaa's spare and evocative poems about his hitch in Vietnam:

He danced with tall grass
for a moment, like he was swaying
with a woman. Our gun barrels
glowed white-hot.
When I got to him,
a blue halo
of flies had already claimed him.

For some of those children who once were lulled to sleep by
the rhythms of Seuss and Sendak, poetry comes now set to music:
Nirvana and Arrested Development, Tori Amos and the Indigo
Girls. Many readers are scared off young, put off by the be-
lief that poetry is difficult and demanding. We complain that it
doesn't sound like the way we talk, but if it sounds like the way
we talk, we complain that it doesn't rhyme.

A poet who teaches in the schools tells of how one boy told
him he couldn't, wouldn't write poetry. Then one day in class he
heard Hayden Carruth's "Cows at Night" and cried, "I didn't
know we were allowed to write poems about cows."

Or write a poem about two women talking in the kitchen.

Crazy as a bessy bug.
Jack wasn't cold
In his grave before
She done up & gave all
The insurance money
To some young pigeon
Who never hit a lick
At work in his life.

He cleaned her out & left
With Donna Faye's girl.
Honey, hush. You don't
Say . . .

That's Mr. Komunyakaa from the collection, *Neon Vernacular*, that won the Pulitzer. His publisher originally printed 2,500 copies, which is fairly large for poetry but a joke to the folks who stock those racks at the airport. Few are the parents who leap up with soundless joy when a son or daughter announces, "Mom, Dad, I've decided to become a poet."

People who are knowledgeable about poetry sometimes discuss it in that knowing, rather hateful way in which enophiles talk about wine: robust, delicate, muscular. This has nothing to do with how most of us experience it, the heart coming around the corner and unexpectedly running into the mind. Of all the words that have stuck to the ribs of my soul, poetry has been the most filling. Robert Frost, Robert Lowell, Elizabeth Bishop, Emily Dickinson, the divine W. B. Yeats. April is the cruelest month. O World, I cannot hold thee close enough! After the first death, there is no other. A terrible beauty is born.

Poems are now appearing on posters in subway trains; one commuter said of a Langston Hughes poem, "I can't express it, but I get it." Now rolling through the soot-black dark of the tunnels and the surprising sunshine where the subways suddenly shoot aboveground: Marianne Moore, William Carlos Williams, Audre Lord, May Swenson, Rita Dove, and Gwendolyn Brooks, who wrote that exquisite evocation of carpe diem, and perhaps of poetry, too:

Exhaust the little moment. Soon it dies.
And be it gash or gold it will not come
Again in this identical disguise.

Says Mr. Komunyakaa, who teaches, "I never really approached it from the perspective of making a living. It was simply a need." Maybe it's a need for us all we just forget.

poems
for
life

Dear Ms. Rabbino,

Thank you for your letter, and I applaud your project as a means to raise funds for the International Rescue Committee to benefit refugee children.

You have asked me to give you a copy of my favorite poem. I have many favorite poems, but I read one the other day that is my current favorite and I thought you might wish to include it in your book. The poem, "In Black Earth, Wisconsin," was written by Andrea Musher. I read it in a recently published anthology of poems by Dane County writers of Wisconsin. The anthology is called *The Glacier Stopped Here*, published by the Dane County Cultural Affairs Commission and Isthmus Publishing Company in 1994.

The poem is my favorite presently because it paints for me a picture of this very specific Wisconsin country. I get a clear picture of the farm, the mother and family and the graveyard at the top of the hill. It evokes for me a particular time and an almost unbearable emotional path that this mother and family have taken.

Poems are perhaps my favorite kind of reading because they encapsulate in a few descriptive lines a world — a world that I may never get to visit but which, somehow, recalls for me the common ground we all stand on.

All the best with your project.

Sincerely,

In Black Earth, Wisconsin

thistles take the hillside
a purple glory of furred spears
a fierce army of spiky weeds
we climb through them
your mother, two of her daughters, and me
a late walk in the long June light

in the barn the heart throb
of the milking machine continues
as your father and brother change
the iodide-dipped tubes
from one udder to the next
and the milk courses through the pipeline
to the cooling vat where it swirls
like a lost sea in a silver box

we are climbing to the grove of white birch trees
whose papery bark will shed
the heart-ringed initials of your sister
as the grief wears down

this farm bears milk and hay
and this mother woman walking beside us
has borne nine children

and one magic one is dead:

                    riding her bike
                    she was a glare of light
                    on the windshield of the car
                    that killed her

a year and a half has passed
and death is folded in among the dishtowels
hangs in the hall closet by the family photos
and like a ring of fine mist
above the dinner table

we stand on a hill looking at birch bark
poking among hundred-year-old graves
that have fallen into the grass
rubbing the moss off and feeling for the names
that the stone sheds
we are absorbing death like nitrates
fertilizing our growth

this can happen:

                    a glare of light
                    an empty place
                    wordlessly we finger her absence
already there are four grandchildren
the family grows thick as thistle

                    — Andrea Musher

Dear Leslie.

Thank you for your letter of April 24th. I think your class project sounds wonderful and I hope it is an enormous success.

My favorite poem is "The Daffodil" by William Wordsworth because it is light-hearted and gay and brings to mind such beautiful images. In the Spring, my garden is filled with golden daffodils which are a glorious sight to behold, and when the winter comes, I can close my eyes and see them "fluttering and dancing in the breeze" and my heart is uplifted and filled with joy. I have enclosed a copy of the poem for your book.

Most Sincerely,

Brooke Astor

Mrs. Vincent Astor

I Wandered Lonely as a Cloud

I wandered lonely as a cloud
That floats on high o'er vales and hills,
When all at once I saw a crowd,
A host, of golden daffodils,
Beside the lake, beneath the trees,
Fluttering and dancing in the breeze.

Continuous as the stars that shine
And twinkle on the milky way,
They stretched in never-ending line
Along the margin of a bay:
Ten thousand saw I at a glance,
Tossing their heads in sprightly dance.

The waves beside them danced, but they
Out-did the sparkling waves in glee:
A poet could not but be gay,
In such a jocund company:
I gazed — and gazed — but little thought
What wealth the show to me had brought:

For oft, when on my couch I lie
In vacant or in pensive mood,
They flash upon that inward eye

Which is the bliss of solitude;
And then my heart with pleasure fills,
And dances with the daffodils.

— William Wordsworth

Dear Maggie,

Among my favorite poems, one is certainly Shelley's "Ode to the West Wind," with its rich optimism: "If Winter comes, can Spring be far behind?"

Read it, and cheer.

Best,

Ken Auletta

ALLEN GINSBERG

Dear Nightingale-Bamford School:

Percy B. Shelley's "Ode to the West Wind" is my favorite poem tonite — because following the phrasings & breaths indicated by punctuation, you can get a high buzz reciting it aloud, & it comes to ecstatic expression of abandon to truth at the end —

Sincerely Allen Ginsberg

ODE TO THE WEST WIND

I

O wild West Wind, thou breath of Autumn's being,
Thou, from whose unseen presence the leaves dead
Are driven, like ghosts from an enchanter fleeing,

Yellow, and black, and pale, and hectic red,
Pestilence-stricken multitudes: O thou,
Who chariotest to their dark wintry bed

The wingèd seeds, where they lie cold and low,
Each like a corpse within its grave, until
Thine azure sister of the Spring shall blow

Her clarion o'er the dreaming earth, and fill
(Driving sweet buds like flocks to feed in air)
With living hues and odors plain and hill:

Wild Spirit, which art moving everywhere;
Destroyer and preserver; hear, oh, hear!

II

Thou on whose stream, mid the steep sky's commotion,
Loose clouds like earth's decaying leaves are shed,
Shook from the tangled boughs of Heaven and Ocean,

Angels of rain and lightning: there are spread
On the blue surface of thine airy surge,
Like the bright hair uplifted from the head

Of some fierce Maenad, even from the dim verge
Of the horizon to the zenith's height,
The locks of the approaching storm. Thou dirge

Of the dying year, to which this closing night
Will be the dome of a vast sepulcher,
Vaulted with all thy congregated might

Of vapors, from whose solid atmosphere
Black rain, and fire, and hail will burst: oh, hear!

III
Thou who didst waken from his summer dreams
The blue Mediterranean, where he lay,
Lulled by the coil of his crystálline streams,

Beside a pumice isle in Baiae's bay,
And saw in sleep old palaces and towers
Quivering within the wave's intenser day,

All overgrown with azure moss and flowers
So sweet, the sense faints picturing them! Thou
For whose path the Atlantic's level powers

Cleave themselves into chasms, while far below
The sea-blooms and the oozy woods which wear
The sapless foliage of the ocean, know

Thy voice, and suddenly grow gray with fear,
And tremble and despoil themselves: oh, hear!

IV

If I were a dead leaf thou mightest bear;
If I were a swift cloud to fly with thee;
A wave to pant beneath thy power, and share

The impulse of thy strength, only less free
Than thou, O uncontrollable! If even
I were as in my boyhood, and could be

The comrade by thy wanderings over Heaven,
As then, when to outstrip thy skyey speed
Scarce seemed a vision; I would ne'er have striven

As thus with thee in prayer in my sore need.
Oh, lift me as a wave, a leaf, a cloud!
I fall upon the thorns of life! I bleed!

A heavy weight of hours has chained and bowed
One too like thee: tameless, and swift, and proud.

V

Make me thy lyre, even as the forest is:
What if my leaves are falling like its own!
The tumult of thy mighty harmonies

Will take from both a deep, autumnal tone,
Sweet though in sadness. Be thou, Spirit fierce,
My spirit! Be thou me, impetuous one!

Drive my dead thoughts over the universe
Like withered leaves to quicken a new birth!
And, by the incantation of this verse,

Scatter, as from an unextinguished hearth
Ashes and sparks, my words among mankind!
Be through my lips to unawakened earth

The trumpet of a prophecy! O Wind,
If Winter comes, can Spring be far behind?

— Percy Bysshe Shelley

Dearest Olivia,

Thank you so much for your note. I'm sorry for the delay. Life has been rather hectic recently.

However, I've enclosed a poem by Langston Hughes called "To Be Somebody." I love this poem because of the inspiration it has given me as an artist struggling, striving and working to make it to the top of my profession. The beauty of the poem is that there is always room for each and every one of us at the top.

Many Thanks, Best Wishes and Great Success.

Sincerely,

Harolyn M. Blackwell

TO BE SOMEBODY

Little girl
Dreaming of a baby grand piano
(Not knowing there's a Steinway bigger, bigger)
Dreaming of a baby grand to play
That stretches paddle-tailed across the floor,
Not standing upright
Like a bad boy in the corner,
But sending music

Up the stairs and down the stairs
And out the door
To confound even Hazel Scott
Who might be passing!

Oh!

Little boy
Dreaming of boxing gloves
Joe Louis wore,
The gloves that sent
Two dozen men to the floor.
Knockout!
Bam! Bop! Mop!

There's always room,
They say,
At the top.

— Langston Hughes

Dear Rebecca,

My poem is —

Laughing Down Lonely Canyons

Fear corrodes my dreams tonight,
and mist has grayed the hills,
mountains seem too tall to climb,
December winds are chill.
There's no comfort on the earth,
I am a child abandoned,
Till I feel your hand in mine
and laugh down lonely canyons.

Snow has bent the trees in grief,
my summer dreams are dead,
Flowers are but ghostly stalks,
the clouds drift dull as lead.
There is no solace in the sky,
I am a child abandoned.
Till we chase the dancing moon
and laugh down lonely canyons.

Birds have all gone south too soon,
and frogs refuse to sing,

Deer lie hidden in the woods,
the trout asleep till spring.
There is no wisdom in the wind —
I am a child abandoned
Till we race across the fields
and laugh down lonely canyons.

Darkness comes too soon tonight,
the trees are silent scars,
rivers rage against the rocks,
and snow conceals the stars.
There's no music in the air
I am a child abandoned
Till I feel my hand in yours
and laugh down lonely canyons.

                    — James Cavenaugh

    To some it may seem soupy — but the images hit me hard
when I first saw it . . . and it comes very close to being lyric — a
thing I am partial to.

                                              Best,

                    Martin Charbin.

Dear Grade V:

I am happy to participate in your project. I have a favorite quotation from a poem called "Outwitted," by Edwin Markham. This particular stanza sums up the strategy of inclusiveness that I employ at every opportunity in my political life:

He drew a circle that shut me out,
Heretic, rebel, a thing to flout.
But Love and I had the wit to win,
We drew a circle that took him in!

I hope this has been useful. Thank you for asking. Best wishes for a successful project.

Sincerely,

Mario M. Cuomo

Dear Rebecca:

It is with pleasure that I respond to your request for my favorite poem for the book that your class is compiling to raise money for refugee children. May I applaud you and your classmates on having chosen to devote yourselves to so worthwhile a project.

In my life, of course, I have read many lovely and moving poems. The one I am sending you seems particularly apt for a book intended to benefit children. "Stars" by the great American poet Langston Hughes is a poem that works on the psyche on several levels at the same time. On one level, it is simply about the beauty of a moment in space and time. On another, it is about the Village of Harlem, a special place with a unique history. On a third level, "Stars" is about having a dream and striving to realize that dream. Finally, the poem evokes the presence and danger of obstacles to achieving our dreams. Moreover, "Stars," like all great works, is one in which new meaning can be uncovered with each reading.

The text of the poem is printed below. Please accept my warm wishes for the success of your humanitarian enterprise.

Sincerely,

STARS

O, sweep of stars over Harlem streets,
O, little breath of oblivion that is night.
A city building
To a mother's song.
A city dreaming
To a lullaby.
Reach up your hand, dark boy, and take a star.
Out of the little breath of oblivion
That is night,
Take just
One star.

— Langston Hughes

Dear Lily,

A poem I have always loved is "A Blessing," by James Wright. I've enclosed a copy here in case you're not familiar with it. In the poem, a man walks into a field to look at two ponies grazing there at twilight. I can't be sure if this is my favorite poem, but I do know that it is one that I return to year after year and say to myself with undiminished awe.

James Wright is an American poet from Ohio who lived until 1980. I knew him when we were students at Kenyon College — he was writing poems even then, as a young man.

My best wishes to you, Lily, and to your classmates. All together you are doing a wonderful thing with your project.

E. L. Doctorow

A Blessing

Just off the highway to Rochester, Minnesota,
Twilight bounds softly forth on the grass.
And the eyes of those two Indian ponies
Darken with kindness.
They have come gladly out of the willows

To welcome my friend and me.
We step over the barbed wire into the pasture
Where they have been grazing all day, alone.
They ripple tensely, they can hardly contain their happiness
That we have come.
They bow shyly as wet swans. They love each other.
There is no loneliness like theirs.
At home once more,
They begin munching the young tufts of spring in the darkness.
I would like to hold the slenderer one in my arms,
For she has walked over to me
And nuzzled my left hand.
She is black and white,
Her mane falls wild on her forehead,
And the light breeze moves me to caress her long ear
That is delicate as the skin over a girl's wrist.
Suddenly I realize
That if I stepped out of my body I would break
Into blossom.

— James Wright

Dear Clare,

I thank you for your letter regarding the work Class V is doing to raise money for the International Rescue Committee.

My favorite poem as a child was Rudyard Kipling's "If." The reason I liked it is because it told me how best to approach life.

Good luck with your project.

Cordially,

DIANE SAWYER

Dear Alexia,

My favorite poem is "If" by Rudyard Kipling. I know it's a little old-fashioned, but it certainly helps when you need a poem as a friend — whether you're "my son" or "my daughter."

Sincerely,

IF —

If you can keep your head when all about you
    Are losing theirs and blaming it on you,
If you can trust yourself when all men doubt you,
    But make allowance for their doubting too;
If you can wait and not be tired by waiting
    Or being lied about, don't deal in lies,
Or being hated don't give way to hating,
    And yet don't look too good, nor talk too wise:

If you can dream — and not make dreams your master;
    If you can think — and not make thoughts your aim:
If you can meet with Triumph and Disaster
    And treat those two imposters just the same;
If you can bear to hear the truth you've spoken
    Twisted by knaves to make a trap for fools,
Or watch the things you gave your life to, broken,
    And stoop and build 'em up with worn-out tools:

If you can make one heap of all your winnings
    And risk it on one turn of pitch-and-toss,
And lose, and start again at your beginnings
    And never breathe a word about your loss;

If you can force your heart and nerve and sinew
    To serve your turn long after they are gone,
And so hold on when there is nothing in you
    Except the Will which says to them: "Hold on!"

If you can talk with crowds and keep your virtue,
    Or walk with Kings — nor lose the common touch,
If neither foes nor loving friends can hurt you,
    If all men count with you, but none too much;
If you can fill the unforgiving minute
    With sixty seconds' worth of distance run,
Yours is the Earth and everything that's in it,
    And — which is more — you'll be a Man, my son!

— Rudyard Kipling

Dear Elaine:

I applaud your efforts on behalf of the International Rescue Committee in order to benefit refugee children, and I am pleased to provide a poem of my choosing. Here, then, is the poem I have chosen.

If I can stop one Heart from breaking
I shall not live in vain
If I can ease one Life the Aching
Or cool one pain

Or help one fainting Robin
Unto his Nest again
I shall not live in Vain.

— Emily Dickinson

I love this poem because of its simplicity and for what it reveals about the author's value system. Emily Dickinson valued service to others as a central purpose in living. In a world that is frequently ruled by selfishness, Emily Dickinson shines like a heavenly star.

Sincerely,

Rudy Giuliani

Dear Antoinette,

I am writing to you in response to your letter of April 27 in which you ask me to share with you a favorite poem and some explanation of why it is my favorite.

Rather than select a whole poem I have selected four lines from T. S. Eliot's *Four Quartets*. These lines come from the last of the *Four Quartets* called "Little Gidding." A copy is enclosed. I like these four lines because they express for me, as a religious person, our going from God and our return to God. Therefore, they are lines which hold a promise. They also express what we could call the innate curiosity of human beings always wanting to explore. But, at the same time, hidden there is our true home.

I hope this arrives on time.

Faithfully,

+ Richard

FROM "LITTLE GIDDING" (*FOUR QUARTETS*)

We shall not cease from exploration
And the end of all our exploring
Will be to arrive where we started
And know the place for the first time.
— T. S. Eliot

Dear Rebecca,

Please excuse my delay in answering your lovely letter —

Your project sounds like an estimable one — anything that gets people interested in poetry at an early age is a wonderful idea. I'm sending along the fragments of two poems (done from memory). The first, from "The Passing of Arthur," I like very much because it reflects the idea of the world as a changing place where people have to adapt constantly to changing truths; it seems a good answer to those who believe that everything done in their childhood is better than anything that has happened since. For me as a reporter who covered the Civil Rights Revolution in the South in the late fifties and early sixties it has particular meaning.

The other — we'd need more of the poem — is from Robert Frost — "Stopping by Woods on a Snowy Evening" — which John Kennedy quoted at about every appearance in his 1960 campaign — and about which I feel considerable nostalgia.

"And I have promises to keep / And miles to go before I sleep."

Best of luck with your project and I hope I get to meet you someday,

[signature]

"THE PASSING OF ARTHUR" (FROM *IDYLLS OF THE KING*)

And slowly answered Arthur from the barge:
"The old order changeth, yielding place to new,
And God fulfills himself in many ways,
Lest one good custom should corrupt the world.
Comfort thyself: what comfort is in me?
I have lived my life, and that which I have done
May He within himself make pure!"

— Alfred, Lord Tennyson

Dear Olivia:

To select one poem from the world's library of great poetry and declare it to be my favorite poem is as daunting a task as choosing one work of prose and claiming it to be the most significant. In the category of favorite poetry there are any number of selections I could make reaching across the ages back to the time of King David in ancient Israel and going forward to the last decade of the twentieth century.

There is a tendency, completely understandable, for people to react especially favorably to literature that was authored in a geographical setting that they know very well. It is from that perspective that I have chosen to respond to your request by submitting, as one of my favorite expressions, a simple poem entitled "Stopping by Woods on a Snowy Evening." The author is Robert Frost, whose literary skill mirrors so clearly the life and labors of rural people who live in New England. My family own a home on a Vermont mountaintop and the scene that Robert Frost evokes in this poem is one with which I am well familiar as I trek through the snow-filled woods on a cold winter's day. I have seen the solitary house and the frozen lake and I have heard the sounds of harness bells. I know, as well, that in the beautiful solitude, while walking alone in those woods filled with birch and maple, that I cannot remain there, for there are things still to be done, indeed promises to keep.

Thank you for asking me to contribute to this wonderful

project upon which you are engaging to raise the consciousness of people, so that they will be concerned for refugee children so desperately in need of help.

Yours sincerely,

STOPPING BY WOODS ON A SNOWY EVENING

Whose woods these are I think I know.
His house is in the village though;
He will not see me stopping here
To watch his woods fill up with snow.

My little horse must think it queer
To stop without a farmhouse near
Between the woods and frozen lake
The darkest evening of the year.

He gives his harness bells a shake
To ask if there is some mistake.
The only other sound's the sweep
Of easy wind and downy flake.

The woods are lovely, dark and deep,
But I have promises to keep,
And miles to go before I sleep,
And miles to go before I sleep.

— Robert Frost

Dear Ms. Wolff:

I am very flattered to be asked for my "favorite poem"; and your cause is certainly a worthy one — I do not have a "favorite" poem — there are dozens which fall into that category. But one of my favorites is Walt Whitman's "When I Heard the Learn'd Astronomer," which I have enclosed.

I think the reason that this poem affects me as it does has to do with a deep need on my part to preserve a sense of the mystery, the divinity (if you will) of life. Rather than explaining everything away by dry, cerebral means, there are moments when the intellect is not enough, when the spiritual part of me needs nourishment. That, or something like it, is what this poem says to me — and says it very powerfully.

Good luck with your project!

Cordially,

Sheldon Harnick

WHEN I HEARD THE LEARN'D ASTRONOMER

When I heard the learn'd astronomer,
When the proofs, the figures, were ranged in columns
    before me,
When I was shown the charts and diagrams, to add, divide,
    and measure them,

When I sitting heard the astronomer where he lectured
     with much applause in the lecture-room,
How soon unaccountable I became tired and sick,
Till rising and gliding out I wander'd off by myself,
In the mystical moist night-air, and from time to time,
Look'd up in perfect silence at the stars.

                    — Walt Whitman

Stephanie Greco:

I don't know about a favorite poem but there is one that often haunts my mind. It is grim but beautiful. I'm afraid I can't find it, perhaps you might be able to. It is called "The Yachts" and I think it is by William Carlos Williams. (Good Luck)

All the best with your project,

THE YACHTS

contend in a sea which the land partly encloses
shielding them from the too-heavy blows
of an ungoverned ocean which when it chooses

tortures the biggest hulls, the best man knows
to pit against its beatings, and sinks them pitilessly.
Mothlike in mists, scintillant in the minute

brilliance of cloudless days, with broad bellying sails
they glide to the wind tossing green water
from their sharp prows while over them the crew crawls

ant-like, solicitously grooming them, releasing,
making fast as they turn, lean far over and having
caught the wind again, side by side, head for the mark.

In a well guarded arena of open water surrounded by
lesser and greater craft which, sycophant, lumbering
and flittering follow them, they appear youthful, rare

as the light of a happy eye, live with the grace
of all that in the mind is fleckless, free and
naturally to be desired. Now the sea which holds them

is moody, lapping their glossy sides, as if feeling
for some slightest flaw but fails completely.
Today no race. Then the wind comes again. The yachts

move, jockeying for a start, the signal is set and they
are off. Now the waves strike at them but they are too
well made, they slip through, though they take in canvas.

Arms with hands grasping seek to clutch at the prows.
Bodies thrown recklessly in the way are cut aside.
It is a sea of faces about them in agony, in despair

until the horror of the race dawns staggering the mind,
the whole sea become an entanglement of watery bodies
lost to the world bearing what they cannot hold. Broken,

beaten, desolate, reaching from the dead to be taken up
they cry out, failing, failing! their cries rising
in waves still as the skillful yachts pass over.

— William Carlos Williams

MAN WITH WOODEN LEG ESCAPES PRISON

I like this poem because it introduces young readers to the idea that poems don't have to rhyme, and that poems can tell stories. It has a good message about perseverance and determination and adaptation. Finally, James Tate, who won the Pulitzer Prize for Poetry in 1993, deserves the attention.

Man with wooden leg escapes prison. He's caught.
They take his wooden leg away from him. Each day
he must cross a large hill and swim a wide river
to get to the field where he must work all day on
one leg. This goes on for a year. At the Christmas
Party they give him back his leg. Now he doesn't
want it. His escape is all planned. It requires
only one leg.

— James Tate

Dear Ms. Ellis,

I received your letter and I am delighted to participate in your project to aid the International Rescue Committee.

For me, Edgar Allan Poe's "Annabel Lee" is a poem of sentimentality at its very best. It carries the reader back to a gentler age and turns tragedy into a thing of beauty. It is a gracious love poem.

All the best.

Sincerely,

[signature]

Annabel Lee

It was many and many a year ago,
   In a kingdom by the sea,
That a maiden there lived whom you may know
   By the name of Annabel Lee; —
And this maiden she lived with no other thought
   Than to love and be loved by me.

I was a child and *she* was a child,
   In this kingdom by the sea,
But we loved with a love that was more than love —

I and my Annabel Lee —
With a love that the wingèd seraphs in Heaven
    Coveted her and me.

And this was the reason that, long ago,
    In this kingdom by the sea,
A wind blew out of a cloud, chilling
    My beautiful Annabel Lee;
So that her high-born kinsman came
    And bore her away from me,
To shut her up in a sepulcher
    In this kingdom by the sea.

The angels, not half so happy in Heaven,
    Went envying her and me: —
    Yes! — that was the reason (as all men know,
In this kingdom by the sea)
    That the wind came out of the cloud, by night,
Chilling and killing my Annabel Lee.

But our love it was stronger by far than the love
    Of those who were older than we —
Of many far wiser than we —
    And neither the angels in Heaven above,
Nor the demons down under the sea,
    Can ever dissever my soul from the soul
Of the beautiful Annabel Lee: —

For the moon never beams without bringing me dreams
    Of the beautiful Annabel Lee;
And the stars never rise but I feel the bright eyes
    Of the beautiful Annabel Lee;
And so, all the night-tide, I lie down by the side
Of my darling, — my darling, — my life and my bride,
    In her sepulcher there by the sea —
    In her tomb by the sounding sea.

              — Edgar Allan Poe

KENNETH KOCH

Dear Adie Ellis,

I don't really have one Favorite Poem but quite a lot of favorite poems. Some poems seem so good that there couldn't possibly be any poem better, and then one goes on reading and finds another poem one likes just as well. I think if I started listing my favorite poems, it might fill up your whole book — there would be poems by Shakespeare, John Donne, William Carlos Williams, Wallace Stevens, Keats, Shelley, Byron, Frank O'Hara, and a lot more. Also among my favorite poems are some written by the students I had when I was teaching schoolchildren to write poetry, like this one by Jeff Morley. He was in the fifth grade at Public School 61 in New York when he wrote it, I think in 1968. I had asked my students to write poems that were completely untrue — what I called "Lie Poems." Some children wrote lists of funny, crazy things like "I was born on a blackboard," "I fly to school at 12:00 midnight," or "I am in New York on a flying blueberry" — but Jeff wrote about just one strange, and obviously untrue, experience. There was something about it that seemed true, though —

THE DAWN OF ME:

I was born nowhere
And I live in a tree
I never leave my tree
It is very crowded
I am stacked up right against a bird

But I won't leave my tree
Everything is dark
No light!
I hear the bird sing
I wish I could sing
My eyes, they open
And all around my house
The Sea
Slowly I get down in the water
The cool blue water
Oh and the space
I laugh swim and cry for joy
This is my home
    For Ever

— Jeff Morley

With best wishes,

Kurt Kurt

Dear Class V:

Here's my favorite poem. I like it because it shows the way we should all think — particularly us women.

Jill Krementz

THE LOW ROAD

Alone, you can fight,
you can refuse, you can
take what revenge you can
but they roll over you.

But two people fighting
back to back can cut through
a mob, a snake-dancing file
can break a cordon, an army
can meet an army.

Two people can keep each other
sane, can give support, conviction,
love, massage, hope, sex.
Three people are a delegation,

a committee, a wedge. With four
you can play bridge and start
an organization. With six
you can rent a whole house,
eat pie for dinner with no
seconds, and hold a fund raising party.
A dozen make a demonstration.
A hundred fill a hall.
A thousand have solidarity and your own newsletter;
ten thousand, power and your own paper;
a hundred thousand, your own media;
ten million, your own country.

It goes on one at a time,
It starts when you care
to act, it starts when you do
it again after they said no,
it starts when you say We
and know who you mean, and each
day you mean one more.

— Marge Piercy

Dear Jenny,

Thank you for your letter telling me about your book project to raise money for refugee children. I'm delighted you asked me to be involved.

I've enclosed a copy of "Cuttin' Rushes," a poem by Moira O'Neill, who was an Irish poet. My mother was a recitalist and this was one of her favorite poems. In the old days at social gatherings in Hollywood, everyone would take turns performing for each other. I would sing and my mother would recite poetry. I heard her recite this poem so often I learned it by assimilation!

Yours sincerely,

Angela Lansbury.

CUTTIN' RUSHES

Oh, maybe it was yesterday, or fifty years ago!
    Meself was risin' early on a day for cuttin' rushes.
Walkin' up the Brabla' burn, still the sun was low,
    Now I'd hear the burn run an' then I'd hear the thrushes.

Young, still young! — and drenchin' wet the grass,
  Wet the golden honeysuckle hangin' sweetly down;
Here, lad, here! will ye follow where I pass,
  An' find me cuttin' rushes on the mountain.

Then was it only yesterday, or fifty years or so?
  Rippen' round the bog pools high among the heather,
The hook it made me hand sore, I had to leave it go,
  'Twas he that cut the rushes then for me to bind together.
Come, dear, come! — an' back along the burn
  See the darlin' honeysuckle hangin' like a crown.
Quick, one kiss, — sure, there's some one at the turn!
  "Oh, we're after cuttin' rushes on the mountain."

Yesterday, yesterday, or fifty years ago. . . .
  I waken out o' dreams when I hear the summer thrushes.
Oh, that's the Brabla' burn, I can hear it sing an' flow,
  For all that's fair I'd sooner see a bunch o' green rushes.
Run, burn, run! can ye mind when we were young?
  The honeysuckle hangs above, the pool is dark an' brown:
Sing, burn, sing! can ye mind the song ye sung
  The day we cut the rushes on the mountain?

— Moira O'Neill

Dear Zoe,

Thank you for your kind letter about the project at your school. I applaud your contribution to this noble cause. My favorite poem is "Ode on a Grecian Urn," because beauty has its own truth.
    With warmest wishes, and best of luck with the project,

Ode on a Grecian Urn

I

Thou still unravished bride of quietness,
    Thou foster-child of silence and slow time,
Sylvan historian, who canst thus express
    A flowery tale more sweetly than our rhyme:
What leaf-fringed legend haunts about thy shape
    Of deities or mortals, or of both,
        In Tempe or the dales of Arcady?
What men or gods are these? What maidens loath?
    What mad pursuit? What struggle to escape?
        What pipes and timbrels? What wild ecstasy?

II

Heard melodies are sweet, but those unheard
    Are sweeter; therefore, ye soft pipes, play on;
Not to the sensual ear, but, more endeared,
    Pipe to the spirit ditties of no tone:
Fair youth, beneath the trees, thou canst not leave
    Thy song, nor ever can those trees be bare;
      Bold Lover, never, never canst thou kiss,
Though winning near the goal — yet, do not grieve;
    She cannot fade, though thou hast not thy bliss,
      For ever wilt thou love, and she be fair!

III

Ah, happy, happy boughs! that cannot shed
    Your leaves, nor ever bid the Spring adieu;
And, happy melodist, unwearièd,
    For ever piping songs for ever new;
More happy love! more happy, happy love!
    For ever warm and still to be enjoyed,
      For ever panting, and for ever young;
All breathing human passion far above,
    That leaves a heart high-sorrowful and cloyed,
      A burning forehead, and a parching tongue.

IV

Who are these coming to the sacrifice?
    To what green altar, O mysterious priest,

Lead'st thou that heifer lowing at the skies,
  And all her silken flanks with garlands drest?
What little town by river or sea shore,
  Or mountain-built with peaceful citadel,
    Is emptied of this folk, this pious morn?
And, little town, thy streets for evermore
  Will silent be; and not a soul to tell
    Why thou art desolate, can e'er return.

V

O Attic shape! Fair attitude! with brede
  Of marble men and maidens overwrought,
With forest branches and the trodden weed;
  Thou, silent form, dost tease us out of thought
As doth eternity: Cold Pastoral!
  When old age shall this generation waste,
  Thou shalt remain, in midst of other woe
Than ours, a friend to man, to whom thou say'st,
  Beauty is truth, truth beauty — that is all
    Ye know on earth, and all ye need to know.

— John Keats

Dear Ms. Shaw:

Pls. find attached a copy of my poem "The Dog." I chose it because I could remember it.

Most sincerely yours,

[signature: David Mamet]

THE DOG

THE DOG THE DOG
HE LIVES IN THE MARSH.
HIS BARK IS MUTE
HIS LIFE IS HARSH.
HIS PAWS ARE WET.

— David Mamet

Dear Candice Gorman:

I'm delighted to join in your poetry project and I've chosen as my favorite one by Emily Dickinson, which I sometimes recite by heart at difficult times. It, to me, is the affirmation of the power of human imagination and creativity, the ability not only to imagine words unseen but to empathize with people unknown, souls unmet — a different way of saying that none of us are islands, we all share the human experience.

With all best wishes,

[signature: Jason McManus]

I Never Saw a Moor

I never saw a Moor —
I never saw the Sea —
Yet know I how the Heather looks
And what a Billow be.

I never spoke with God
Nor visited in Heaven —
Yet certain am I of the spot
As if the Checks were given —

— Emily Dickinson

Dear Louise,

What a pleasure it is for me to have a letter from you and to hear about the class's wonderful poetry project! I especially admire all this work for refugee children and I am happy to be a part of it.

There are two different poems that are a part of my life. One is in my wallet and has been since I can't remember when.

Life is mostly froth and bubble,
Two things stand like stone;
Kindness in another's trouble,
Courage in your own.

— A. L. Gordon

The other I read for the first time when I was in college, and I copied it then. It beautifully says what I deeply believe, that love is the center of our lives and being.

He that loveth, flieth, runneth, and rejoiceth;
He is free and not "bound". . .
Love feels no burden, thinks nothing of trouble,
Attempts what is above its strength
Pleads no excuse of impossibility . . .
For it thinks all things possible.
It is therefore able to undertake all things, and it
Completes many things, and brings them to a conclusion,
Where he who does not love, faints and lies down.

— Thomas à Kempis

Please put in my order for the book when it is ready, and meanwhile this brings love and admiration for all of you for fine work on behalf of refugee youngsters.

Affectionately,

Joan S. M. Menarin

Dear Elizabeth,

Thank you for your letter and for asking me to choose a poem for your collection. My choice is "Dover Beach" by Matthew Arnold. My explanation for this choice is that it was the first poem I read in English (my fourth language) with any degree of understanding, and it was the subject of one of my first papers for an English literature class. I've reread it many times since with increasing pleasure. Also Matthew Arnold was a great figure at Balliol College, Oxford, where I was an undergraduate, and I belonged to a society named after him.

Next time we are in the elevator together, please do introduce yourself.

With warm good wishes,

Yours sincerely,

W

P.S. We are just leaving for Maine for the summer, so I don't have a copy of the poem to hand, but I'm sure you can find it in any number of anthologies.

DOVER BEACH

The sea is calm tonight.
The tide is full, the moon lies fair
Upon the straits; — on the French coast the light
Gleams and is gone; the cliffs of England stand,
Glimmering and vast, out in the tranquil bay.
Come to the window, sweet is the night-air!
Only, from the long line of spray
Where the sea meets the moon-blanched land,
Listen! You hear the grating roar
Of pebbles which the waves draw back, and fling,
At their return, up the high strand,
Begin, and cease, and then again begin,
With tremulous cadence slow, and bring
The eternal note of sadness in.

Sophocles long ago
Heard it on the Aegean, and it brought
Into his mind the turbid ebb and flow
Of human misery; we
Find also in the sound a thought,
Hearing it by this distant northern sea.

The Sea of Faith
Was once, too, at the full, and round earth's shore

Lay like the folds of a bright girdle furled.
But now I only hear
Its melancholy, long, withdrawing roar,
Retreating, to the breath
Of the night-wind, down the vast edges drear
And naked shingles of the world.

Ah, love, let us be true
To one another! for the world, which seems
To lie before us like a land of dreams,
So various, so beautiful, so new,
Hath really neither joy, nor love, nor light,
Nor certitude, nor peace, nor help for pain;
And we are here as on a darkling plain
Swept with confused alarms of struggle and flight,
Where ignorant armies clash by night.

— Matthew Arnold

Dear Ms. Boulanger,

Further to your letter dated March 1st regarding the book of poems which your class is compiling, I am pleased to enclose the following poem by Faiz Ahmed Faiz which Ismail Merchant has asked that I forward to you:

SONG

Pain will cease, do not grieve, do not grieve —
Friends will return, the heart will rest, do not
    grieve —
The wound will be made whole, do not grieve, do not grieve —
Day will come forth, do not grieve, do not grieve —
The cloud will open, night will decline, do not
    grieve —
The seasons will change, do not grieve, do not grieve.

Ismail Merchant asked me to tell you: "This poem expresses the philosophy of my life. There is always a dawn that we can look forward to."

Sincerely,
Melissa Chung

Dear Ali:

I am honored by your invitation to help you in raising funds for the International Rescue Committee, and delighted by your request for a favorite poem.

Notice that I referred to "a" favorite; that's because I believe one can no more have a single favorite poem than your teachers can have a single favorite student. I love different poems for different reasons, in the same way that your teachers love you.

I'm sending you a copy of Robert Frost's "The Gift Outright" because it contains the elements I like best in Frost's poetry: his use of clean, simple language and commonplace imagery to evoke powerful and complex ideas and emotions. Also, it describes some of the tensions that are part of our roles as Americans and our struggle for democracy.

My best wishes go to you and your classmates on this ambitious and imaginative publishing venture.

Sincerely,

THE GIFT OUTRIGHT

The land was ours before we were the land's.
She was our land more than a hundred years

Before we were her people. She was ours
In Massachusetts, in Virginia,
But we were England's, still colonials,
Possessing what we still were unpossessed by,
Possessed by what we now no more possessed.
Something we were withholding made us weak
Until we found out that it was ourselves
We were withholding from our land of living,
And forthwith found salvation in surrender.
Such as we were we gave ourselves outright
(The deed of gift was many deeds of war)
To the land vaguely realizing westward,
But still unstoried, artless, unenhanced,
Such as she was, such as she would become.

— Robert Frost

Dear Lauren Friedman,

I have too many favorite poems! But since this is for a good cause I will choose one. This sonnet by Mr. Keats has many things in it: fear, desire, ambition, poetic urges, love, despair and much more. Keats was as pure a poet as there was. When I read his words I feel the dead leaves inside me being stirred up; this is what *good* poetry does.

With hopes for your success—

Yours,

Susan Minot

Susan Minot

WHEN I HAVE FEARS THAT I MAY CEASE TO BE

When I have fears that I may cease to be
   Before my pen has glean'd my teeming brain,
Before high-piled books, in charactry,
   Hold like rich garners the full-ripen'd grain;
When I behold, upon the night's starr'd face,
   Huge cloudy symbols of romance,
And think that I may never live to trace
   Their shadows, with the magic hand of chance;
And when I feel, fair creature of an hour,
   That I shall never look upon thee more,
Never have relish in the faery power
   Of unreflecting love; — then on the shore
Of the wide world I stand alone, and think
Till love and fame to nothingness do sink.

                  — John Keats

Ontario Review

Dear Gena Hamshaw:

I choose this poem because it is succinct,
brilliant, and profound in its wisdom.

> Tell all the Truth but tell it slant--
> Success in Circuit lies--
> Too bright for our infirm Delight
> The Truth's superb surprise
>
> As Lightning to the Children eased
> With explanation kind
> The Truth must dazzle gradually
> Or every man be blind--
>
> Emily Dickinson

Good luck with your project!

Sincerely,

Joyce Carol Oates

Dear Laura,

Thank you for your letter about the project to raise money for the International Rescue Committee. I think it's great that you're helping with it, and I'm glad you invited me to choose a favorite poem for the anthology.

Actually, there are a lot of poems that could qualify as my favorite, depending on how I'm feeling at the moment. But I've picked Frank O'Hara's "A Step Away from Them," a poem that I've loved ever since I first read it more than thirty years ago. I like the way the poem uses everyday talk to describe a real guy out walking around looking at things on his lunch hour. This is probably the first time a cheeseburger got into a poem! I also like the way the poem is both light and serious at the same time. It all makes me feel happy, as though I had been lucky enough to get to walk around with the poet.

With best wishes,

Ron Padgett

A STEP AWAY FROM THEM

It's my lunch hour, so I go
for a walk among the hum-colored
cabs. First, down the sidewalk

where laborers feed their dirty
glistening torsos sandwiches
and Coca-Cola, with yellow helmets
on. They protect them from falling
bricks, I guess. Then onto the
avenue where skirts are flipping
above heels and blow up over
grates. The sun is hot, but the
cabs stir up the air. I look
at bargains in wristwatches. There
are cats playing in sawdust.
                              On
to Times Square, where the sign
blows smoke over my head, and higher
the waterfall pours lightly. A
Negro stands in a doorway with a
toothpick, languorously agitating.
A blonde chorus girl clicks: he
smiles and rubs his chin. Everything
suddenly honks: it is 12:40 of
a Thursday.
                    Neon in daylight is a
great pleasure, as Edwin Denby would
write, as are light bulbs in daylight.
I stop for a cheeseburger at JULIET'S
CORNER. Giulietta Masina, wife of

Federico Fellini, *è bell' attrice.*
And chocolate malted. A lady in
foxes on such a day puts her poodle
in a cab.

There are several Puerto
Ricans on the avenue today, which
makes it beautiful and warm. First
Bunny died, then John Latouche,
then Jackson Pollock. But is the
earth as full as life was full, of them?
And one has eaten and one walks,
past the magazines with nudes
and the posters for BULLFIGHT and
the Manhattan Storage Warehouse,
which they'll soon tear down. I
used to think they had the Armory
Show there.

A glass of papaya juice
and back to work. My heart is in my
pocket, it is Poems by Pierre Reverdy.

— Frank O'Hara

Dear Maggie Steele:

This is a poem written by Thomas Wolfe for his posthumously published novel *You Can't Go Home Again.*

EXCERPT FROM "CREDO"

Something has spoken to me in the night,
burning the tapers of the waning year;
something has spoken in the night,
and told me I shall die, I know not where.
Saying:

"To lose the earth you know, for greater
knowing; to lose the life you have, for
greater life; to leave the friends you loved,
for greater loving; to find a land more kind
than home, more large than earth —

"— Whereon the pillars of this earth are
founded, toward which the conscience of the
world is tending — a wind is rising, and the
rivers flow."

Best wishes to you and your publication.

Sincerely,

Harold Prince

Dear Zoe,

When I first received your letter, I wondered if trying to choose a favorite poem, even a favorite poet, was not a little like choosing your favorite child. Poetry has stoked my soul on so many occasions, over so many years, that the assignment seems impossible. And my answer may be dependent on the seasons or my mood. On certain days I swear by the black visions of Dylan Thomas, on others the quiet sensibility of Emily Dickinson. I've learned so much from Robert Lowell and Howard Nemerov, and I never cease to marvel at John Donne and Ezra Pound. In fact, one of my favorite ways to pass an afternoon is paging through a thick two-volume set I've owned for years called *Chief Modern Poets of Britain and America*. It's filled with marginalia and comments.

Looking over it, I come reluctantly to a favorite. The poetry of W. B. Yeats is so filled with quiet passion, not only in the emotional content but in the choice of language in his poems, that I come back to his work over and over again. And my favorite is the poem I used to dedicate my last book to my three children. It seems to me the perfect expression of our wish to give to our loved ones all that is in our hearts and minds:

HE WISHES FOR THE CLOTHS OF HEAVEN

Had I the heavens' embroidered cloths,
Enwrought with golden and silver light,
The blue and the dim and the dark cloths

Of night and light and the half-light,
I would spread the cloths under your feet:
But I, being poor, have only my dreams;
I have spread my dreams under your feet;
Tread softly because you tread on my dreams.

Say this one aloud. It is magic, pure music in the way it lifts, falls, and illuminates.

My very best,

Anna Quindlen

Dear Molly,

I like your idea of the book of poems. If it's not too late I would like to contribute one of my favorites. It's John Donne's sonnet beginning, "Batter my heart, three-personed God." I love its powerful expression of God's grace — so different from so much sloppy, religious verse!

I am spending the summer in Mallorca where we have an old farm house. I'm also adrift for lack of good correspondence — no sarcasm, nor many reference books, etc. We are near the town where George Sand entertained Chopin. I hope this finally reaches you and with it send best wishes for the success of the poetry book.

HOLY SONNET XIV

Batter my heart, three-personed God; for you
As yet but knock, breathe, shine, and seek to mend;
That I may rise and stand, o'erthrow me, and bend
Your force, to break, blow, burn, and make me new.
I, like an usurped town, to another due,
Labor to admit You, but Oh, to no end!
Reason, Your viceroy in me, me should defend,

But is captived, and proves weak or untrue.
Yet dearly I love You, and would be loved fain.
But am betrothed unto Your enemy:
Divorce me, untie, or break that knot again,
Take me to You, imprison me, for I,
Except You enthrall me, never shall be free,
Nor ever chaste, except You ravish me.

— John Donne

THE SECRETARY OF EDUCATION
WASHINGTON

Dear Celene,

Thank you for your letter of June 15. I am pleased to have an opportunity to help with the project to benefit refugee children by sharing my favorite poem with your class.

It is a poem entitled "Duty Was Joy," written by an Indian poet named Tagore:

I slept and dreamt
That life was joy —
I awoke and found
That life was duty —
I acted and behold
Duty was joy.

Very simply, it is meaningful to me because it ties responsibility and action to happiness in life. I share this view, and find that my duties and responsibilities give me great joy.

Sincerely,

Dick Riley

Dear Chloe,

Here is my latest favorite poem. I cannot tell you, in fact, which is my favorite one. I love too many. But the one I am enclosing in this note to you is my latest love.

Dustin Hoffman gave it to me. I don't know who wrote it. He was going to read it at an AIDS benefit. I am worried about sending you a poem which begs people to "Always be drunk," but note the last verse: "Go get yourselves drunk and don't stop. With wine, with poetry, or with virtue, with whatever works best." *Please* be drunk with virtue or poetry!!!! *Forget wine!!!* This is meant to be a poem to encourage passion. My recommendation is to have passion — but not wine. On this point I have to disagree with the writer — so be good!

Have a good summer and thanks.

Isabella Rossellini

From *Le Spleen de Paris*

XXXIII
GET YOURSELF DRUNK

Always be drunk. That's all there is to it: nothing else matters. If you don't want to feel the horrible burden of Time crushing your shoulders and forcing you down, you have to get yourself drunk and not stop.

Drunk with what? With wine, with poetry, with virtue, with whatever works best. Just get yourself drunk.

And if you ever wake up on the front steps of some palace, on the green grass of some ditch, in the lonely gloom of your room, and find that inebriation has faded or disappeared, ask the wind, the wave, the star, the bird, the clock, anything that flees, anything that moans, anything that moves, anything that sings, anything that speaks — ask what time it is; and the wind, the wave, the star, the bird, the clock, will answer: "Time to get yourselves drunk! If you don't want to be the martyred slaves of Time, go get yourselves drunk, get yourselves drunk and don't stop. With wine, with poetry, or with virtue, with whatever works best."

— Charles Baudelaire

Dear Erica,

Here is a poem which made a deep impression on me and which I'll always remember. It's by Siegfried Sassoon, an English poet who fought and was decorated and wounded in the first Great World War, 1914–18. I think of it as the most meaningful anti-war poem I've ever read.

DOES IT MATTER?

Does it matter? — losing your legs? . . .
For people will always be kind,
And you need not show that you mind
When others come in after hunting
To gobble their muffins and eggs.

Does it matter — losing your sight? . . .
There's such splendid work for the blind;
And people will always be kind,
As you sit on the terrace remembering
And turning your face to the light.

Do they matter — those dreams from the pit? . . .
You can drink and forget and be glad,
And people won't say that you're mad;

For they'll know that you've fought for your country,
And no one will worry a bit.
 — Siegfried Sassoon

Sincerely,

Bruce Sales.

To The Nightingale-Bamford School:

This is one of my favorite poems because it confirms the importance of spending time with nature to give beauty and balance to your life. There is nothing more refreshing to the spirit than a walk in the country — whether in the woods or across fields or even along red-rock canyons of the Southwest.

Sincerely,

W Seymour Jr

FROM "INSCRIPTION FOR THE ENTRANCE TO A WOOD"

Stranger, if thou hast learned a truth which needs
No school of long experience, that the world
Is full of guilt and misery, and hast seen
Enough of all its sorrows, crimes, and cares,
To tire thee of it, enter the wild wood
And view the haunts of Nature. The calm shade
Shall bring a kindred calm, and the sweet breeze
That makes the green leaves dance, shall waft a balm
To thy sick heart.

— William Cullen Bryant

Dear Fernanda Winthrop and Class V of
The Nightingale-Bamford School:

Thank you for asking me to be a part of the project *Lifelines*. It's
an honor. I should say the project inspired by *Lifelines*, I suppose,
which was a beautiful gesture to aid needy people and children
in Africa. Because your project focuses on the International Res-
cue Committee to benefit refugee children I chose a poem which I
feel speaks to the possibilities of life. It is by my favorite poet,
Alice Walker. I think she speaks to the potential transformation
we all have inside ourselves. The poem also expresses a hunger
for spiritual liberation and a deep love for Life.

A poem of Ms. Walker's must be included in this collection
because she is such an inspiring, heroic figure to people all over
the world: a beautiful writer, a political figure, a strong propo-
nent for change. Thank you once again for this opportunity.

Sincerely,

ON STRIPPING BARK FROM MYSELF
(FOR JANE, WHO SAID TREES DIE FROM IT)

because women are expected to keep silent about
their close escapes I will not keep silent
and if I am destroyed (naked tree!) someone will
                    please
mark the spot
where I fall and know I could not live
silent in my own lies
hearing their "how *nice* she is!"
whose adoration of the retouched image
I so despise.

No. I am finished with living
for what my mother believes
for what my brother and father defend
for what my lover elevates
for what my sister, blushing, denies or rushes
to embrace.

I find my own
small person
a standing self
against the world
an equality of wills
I finally understand.

My struggle was always against
an inner darkness: I carry within myself
the only known keys
to my death — to unlock life, or close it shut
forever. A woman who loves wood grains, the cold
    yellow
and the sun, I am happy to fight
all outside murderers
as I see I must.

— Alice Walker

Dear Alison,

This is not a poem — but it's my favorite "prose." I carry a copy in my wallet. There's nothing wrong with trying and not succeeding. It's very wrong not to try at all.

Good luck!

Beverly Sills

 It is not the critic who counts, not the man who points out how the strong man stumbled, or where the doer of deeds could have done them better. The credit belongs to the man who is actually in the arena; whose face is marred by dust and sweat and blood; who strives valiantly; who errs and comes short again and again; who knows the great enthusiasms; the great devotions; and spends himself in a worthy cause; who, at the best, knows in the end the triumph of high achievement; and who, at the worst, if he fails, at least fails while daring greatly, so that his place shall never be with those cold and timid souls who know neither victory nor defeat.

— Theodore Roosevelt

Dear Antoinette Grannum,

This project of yours and your classmates sounds like a worthwhile one and I am pleased to send you *My Creed*, which I have used for many years to live by. I hope this will serve your purpose and wish you well in the future.

Sincerely,

Margaret Chase Smith

MY CREED

My creed is that public service must be more than doing a job efficiently and honestly. It must be a complete dedication to the people and to the nation with full recognition that every human being is entitled to courtesy and consideration, that constructive criticism is not only to be expected but sought, that smears are not only to be expected but fought, that honor is to be earned but not bought.

— Margaret Chase Smith

Dear Lindsay Richardson —

I have no "favorite" poem, but a short one that I like immensely is by Christopher Logue. Here it is:

> Come to the edge.
> We might fall.
> Come to the edge.
> It's too high!
> COME TO THE EDGE!
> So they came
> and he pushed
> and they flew.

As a writer, I think this is the most succinct description of the relationship between the artist and the audience (or viewer or listener) that I've ever read.

Yours sincerely,

Stephen Sondheim

Dear Class V:

My favorite is John Donne's Meditation #17, "No Man Is an Island."

The poem is especially meaningful because to live is to learn the truth that no man is an island — and that we must respect others as we would ourselves want to be respected.

Liv Ullmann

Meditation #17

No man is an island, entire of itself; every man is a piece of the continent, a part of the main; if a clod be washed away by the sea, Europe is the less, as well as if a promontory were, as well as if a manor of thy friends or of thine own were; any man's death diminishes me, because I am involved in mankind; and therefore never send to know for whom the bell tolls; it tolls for thee.

— John Donne

Dear Emma —

I congratulate you and your class for wanting to do something about world hunger.

A poem I often quote in lectures is this one by William Blake:

The Angel that presided o'er my birth
Said, "Little creature, form'd of Joy & Mirth,
Go love without the help of any Thing on Earth."

That's the whole thing, Emma, but it seems to me that there is a whole lot there, if you stop to think about it. It says to me that loving people are born that way, and don't need any prods or rewards to make them helpful, compassionate and affectionate.

I sometimes paraphrase it ever so slightly when talking to people who want to be writers and who need advice. In the third line I substitute "write" for "love."

Cheers,

Dear Leslie —

I am enclosing the first lines of "The Ancient Mariner," which I had to memorize in 8th grade at The Brooklyn Ethical Culture School. Actually, I still have friends from that time and when we get together, at some point we begin to recite "The Ancient Mariner," which is odd for girls from Brooklyn! He will always be dear and close to my heart.

Wendy Wasserstein

FROM "THE RIME OF THE ANCIENT MARINER"

Part I
It is an ancient Mariner,
And he stoppeth one of three.
"By thy long grey beard and glittering eye,
Now whereof stopp'st thou me?

The Bridegroom's doors are opened wide,
And I am next of kin;
The guests are met, the feast is set:
May'st hear the merry din."

He holds him with his skinny hand,
"There was a ship," quoth he.

"Hold off! unhand me, grey-beard loon!"
Eftsoons his hand dropt he.

He holds him with his glittering eye —
The Wedding-Guest stood still,
And listens like a three years' child:
The Mariner hath his will.

The Wedding-Guest sat on a stone:
He cannot choose but hear;
And thus spake on that ancient man,
The bright-eyed Mariner.

— Samuel Taylor Coleridge

Dear Nicole,

My choice of poem for your compilation would be Rupert Brooke's "Clouds." I haven't got a copy of it on hand, but you shouldn't have any trouble tracking it down. Please do forgive me for not finding it myself; things are a bit hectic at the moment and I am leaving to do some research in the Arctic tomorrow. The opening line of the poem is "Down the blue night the unending columns press." Rupert Brooke was an Englishman who died during the First World War. He writes with innocence and beauty which I believe were permanently extinguished by that war, and that makes his words all the more poignant to me. "Clouds" was the first poem I ever voluntarily memorized, so it has always been a favorite of mine.

Best of luck with your project. It truly is a worthy cause.

Yours —

Paul Watkins

CLOUDS

Down the blue night the unending columns press
  In noiseless tumult, break and wave and flow,
  Now tread the far South, or lift rounds of snow

Up to the white moon's hidden loveliness.
Some pause in their grave wandering comradeless,
   And turn with profound gesture vague and slow,
   As who would pray good for the world, but know
Their benediction empty as they bless.

They say that the Dead die not, but remain
   Near to the rich heirs of their grief and mirth.
     I think they ride the calm mid-heaven, as these,

In wise majestic melancholy train,
   And watch the moon, and the still-raging seas,
And men, coming and going on the earth.

                 — Rupert Brooke

Dear Sophia,

Thanks for your letter. I am always happy to hear from young people.

Of course, I think your poetry project is worthwhile (in fact, I am a vice-president of the International Rescue Committee), and therefore I am enclosing a poem for you. It's by a boy named Motele — and was originally written in Yiddish, which was the language of my childhood as well. I have always found it moving.

With best wishes —

Eliy Wsf

From tomorrow on, I shall be sad —
From tomorrow on!
Today I will be gay.

What is the use of sadness — tell me that? —
Because these evil winds begin to blow?
Why should I grieve for tomorrow — today?
Tomorrow may be so good, so sunny,
Tomorrow the sun may shine for us again;
We shall no longer need to be sad.

From tomorrow on, I shall be sad —
From tomorrow on!
Not today; no! today I will be glad.
And every day, no matter how bitter it be,
I will say:
From tomorrow on, I shall be sad,
Not today!

— Motele

Dear Erica,

Thank you for your letter which I am confused to see is dated June 9, 1993. I received it last week! I wonder if you still wish to receive a poem for your International Rescue Committee book. If so, here is one of my favorite poems. I love it because it reminds us that all the people of the earth belong to one family. Good luck with your project.

Best Wishes,
Elizabeth Winthrop

WILD GEESE

You do not have to be good.
You do not have to walk on your knees
for a hundred miles through the desert, repenting.
You only have to let the soft animal of your body
     love what it loves.
Tell me about despair, yours, and I will tell you mine.
Meanwhile the world goes on.
Meanwhile the sun and the clear pebbles of the rain
are moving across the landscapes,
over the prairies and the deep trees,
the mountains and the rivers.
Meanwhile the wild geese, high in the clean blue air
are heading home again.

Whoever you are, no matter how lonely,
the world offers itself to your imagination,
calls to you like the wild geese, harsh and exciting —
over and over announcing your place
in the family of things.

— Mary Oliver

Dear Miss Kalayjian,

I must confess that the poem I most often recite to myself and anyone who will listen is Noel Coward's "I've Been to a Marvelous Party." Why? I can't explain it. The sheer aimless rollicking silliness of it just appeals to me. I offer a sample stanza:

I've been to a marvelous party,
I must say the fun was intense,
We all had to do
What the people we knew
Would be doing a hundred years hence.
Dear Cecil arrived wearing armor,
Some shells and a black feather boa,
Poor Millicent wore a surrealist comb
Made of bits of mosaic from St. Peter's in Rome,
But the weight was so great that she had to go home,
I couldn't have liked it more!

— Noel Coward

With best wishes,

Tom Wolfe

Grade V, 1992–93

Christine Alicea
Kate Auletta
Sasha Bernstein
Melissa Butler
Katherine Clifford
Rachel Coll
Louisa Conrad
Clare Cosman
Enerria Edmond
Adrienne Ellis
Amber Ellis
Alexandra Hagerty
Eugenia Hamshaw
Rebecca Hessel
Margot Hill
Samantha Hill
Lara Kalayjian
Louise Lamphere
Kathryn Lawton
Carah Lucas-Hill
Celene Menschel
Lee Katherine Miller
Hillary Nammack

Elizabeth Niemiec
Chloe Polemis
Lindsay Richardson
Annabelle Saks
Kristina Scurry
Zoe Settle
Emma Sheanshang
Ginger Shields
Margarette Steele
Rebecca Tanenbaum
Cara Thomas
Allison Toombs
Stefanie Victor
Ellison Ward
Alison Weisser
Laura Wheater
Fernanda Winthrop
Erica Wolff
Deborah Wolfson
Karen Yeung

Grade V, 1993–94

Agnes Ahlander
Nicole Arens

Elaine Blanck
Adriana Boulanger
Lia Brezavar
Carolyn Centeno
Francesca Forrestal
Lauren Friedman
Juliet Fuisz
Candice Gorman
Antoinette Grannum
Stephanie Greco
Laura Hampton
Alexia Jacobs
Shanthini Kasturi
Leslie Kaufmann
Olivia Kirby
Emily Kracauer
Hillary Matlin
Alfia Muzio
Evelyn Ngeow
Alexandra Odevall
Jean Petrek-Duban
Anne Rabbino
Elana Rakoff
Margaret Ross
Molly Shaw
Anne Stephenson

Cecile St. Hilaire
Jenny Tolan
Alexis Versandi
Lily Vonnegut
Elettra Wiedemann
Sophia Withers
Venetia Young

Contributors

Jane Alexander is an actress and author who served as the director of the National Endowment for the Arts. She won a Tony award for *The Great White Hope* and has appeared in a number of films.

Brooke Astor was president of the Vincent Astor Foundation and corporate board member of the Astor Home for Children. Her books include *Patchwork Child*, *Footprints*, and *The Last Blossom on the Plum Tree*. Astor passed away in 2007.

Ken Auletta is a columnist for *The New Yorker* and the author of national bestsellers, including *Googled; Three Blind Mice: How the TV Networks Lost Their Way;* and *Greed and Glory on Wall Street.*

Harolyn M. Blackwell is a lyric coloratura who made her debut at the Metropolitan Opera in 1994 and achieved renown for her roles in *Die Fledermaus* and *Daughter of the Regiment.* She has sung at the White House and with many national opera companies.

Martin Charnin won a Tony award for his lyrics to *Annie*, which he directed on Broadway. He also directed *The First* and *A Little Family Business* and is the author of *The Giraffe Like Ole Blue Eyes*, a children's book. He passed away in 2019.

Mario Cuomo was governor of New York State from 1982 to 1994. He was the author of *The New York Idea: An Experiment in Democracy* and coeditor of *Lincoln on Democracy.* Cuomo also wrote a children's book based on his own experiences called *The Blue Spruce.* He passed away in 2015.

David Dinkins was mayor of New York City from 1988 to 1992 and subsequently taught at Columbia University. He passed away in 2020.

E. L. Doctorow's works include *Ragtime*, *The Book of Daniel*, *World's*

Fair, Billy Bathgate, The March, Welcome to Hard Times, and Homer & Langley. He received numerous awards including the the National Book Award, National Book Critics Circle Award, and National Humanities Medal. Doctorow passed away in 2015.

Geraldine Ferraro was the first woman to run for the vice presidency of the United States. Author of *Changing History: Women, Power, and Politics*, she was appointed to the United Nations Human Rights Commission Conference in 1993. Ferraro passed away in 2011.

Allen Ginsberg's iconic poetry defined the Beat Generation. He passed away in 1997. Nearly all of his works remain in print.

Rudolph Giuliani was the mayor of New York City from 1994 to 2001. He also ran for the Republican Party nomination in the 2008 United States presidential election.

Richard F. Grein was bishop of the Episcopal Church of New York City, and is coauthor of *Preparing Younger Children for First Communion*. Now retired, Bishop Grein serves as Bishop-in-Residence at St. Mark's Episcopal Church in New Canaan, Connecticut.

David Halberstam was a Pulitzer Prize–winning journalist known for his coverage of Vietnam and the Civil Rights Movement. He passed away in 2007.

Sheldon Harnick is an American lyricist who won Tony awards for his lyrics to *Fiddler on the Roof* and *Fiorello!*

Bill Irwin is a clown, dancer, and stage and film actor whose Broadway credits include *Largely New York*, *The Regard of Flight*, and *Fool Moon*. He has won Tony awards for his performances in *Largely New York* and *Who's Afraid of Virginia Woolf?*

Peter Jennings was the anchor and senior editor of *ABC World News Tonight*, and co-anchor of *Turning Point*, ABC News. He passed away in 2005.

Edward I. Koch was mayor of New York City from 1978 to 1989. He was the author of *His Eminence and Hizzoner* and *Citizen Koch* and coauthor of a children's book based on his own experiences called *Eddie, Harold's Little Brother*. He passed away in 2013.

Kenneth Koch, poet and playwright, taught at Columbia University. His works include *Wishes, Lies, and Dreams: Teaching Children to Write Poetry*, and *Rose, Where Did You Get That Red? Teaching Poetry to Children*. In 1996, Koch was inducted into the American Academy of Arts and Letters. He passed away in 2002.

Jill Krementz is a photographer and author whose works include *The Face of South Vietnam; Sweet Pea: A Black Girl Growing Up in the Rural South;* and *Lily Goes to the Playground*.

Angela Lansbury is a five-time Tony award–winning actress and singer who most recently starred in Broadway revivals of *Blithe Spirit* and *A Little Night Music*.

Yo-Yo E. Ma is a cellist who has performed with Pablo Casals, Isaac Stern, Leonard Bernstein, and orchestras throughout the world. Among many awards, Ma won the National Medal of Arts in 2001 and the Presidential Medal of Freedom in 2011.

David Mamet's award-winning plays include *Glengarry Glen Ross*, *Speed the Plow*, and *Oleanna*. He is also the author of *Warm and Cold*, *The Village*, and *The Hero Pony* and a filmmaker whose movies include *Heist, House of Games*, and *The Winslow Boy*.

Jason McManus was editor-in-chief of *Time* magazine from 1988 to 1994 and the author of a collection of short stories. He passed away in 2019.

Joan S. McMenamin was headmistress of The Nightingale-Bamford School from 1971 to 1992 and was a member of the board of trustees of Roberts College in Istanbul and the English Speaking Union. She passed away in 2004.

Ved Mehta was a staff writer for *The New Yorker* and the author of *Portrait of India, The Stolen Light*, and *Up at Oxford*. He passed away in 2021.

Ismail Merchant produced many award-winning films, including *A Room with a View*, *Howards End*, and *The Remains of the Day*. He and partner James Ivory headed Merchant Ivory films for over forty years. He passed away in 2005.

Ruth W. Messinger was Manhattan Borough president from 1990 to 1998, served on the New York City Council for twelve years, and was CEO of Jewish World Service from 1998 to 2016.

Susan Minot is a writer whose works include *Monkeys*, *Folly*, and most recently, *Why I Don't Write*. Among other honors, she has received an O. Henry Prize and a Pushcart Prize for her work.

Joyce Carol Oates is the author of many novels including *A Garden of Earthly Delights*, *Wonderland*, *Black Water*, *We Were the Mulvaneys*, *The Gravedigger's Daughter*, and *Them*, which received the National Book Award in 1970. Since 1978, she has been teaching at Princeton University.

Ron Padgett was the director of publications at Teachers & Writers Collaborative, an editor at *Teachers & Writers Magazine*, and the founder of Full Court Press.

Harold Prince, winner of over twenty Tony Awards, produced *Pajama Game*, *Damn Yankees*, and *West Side Story*, and directed *Phantom of the Opera*, *Kiss of the Spiderwoman*, and *Show Boat*. He passed away in 2019.

Anna Quindlen is a Pulitzer Prize–winning journalist and bestselling author. She worked as a columnist at the *New York Times* before leaving to write full time.

David Read was a chaplain to the forces of the British army during the Second World War and served as senior minister of Madison Avenue Presbyterian Church in New York City from 1956 to 1989. He passed away in 2001.

Richard W. Riley was formerly governor of South Carolina and served as U.S. Secretary of Education under President Bill Clinton.

Isabella Rossellini is a model and actress whose films include *White Nights*, *Blue Velvet*, *Wild at Heart*, and *Fearless*.

Gene Saks was a Tony Award–winning director who helmed *Half a Sixpence*, *Mame*, and *Same Time, Next Year*. His film credits include *The Odd Couple* and *Barefoot in the Park*. He passed away in 2015.

Diane Sawyer was a correspondent on CBS's *60 Minutes*, co-anchor of *Prime Time Live*, ABC News, and *Good Morning America*, and host of *ABC World News*.

Whitney North Seymour Jr. was a New York trial lawyer, federal prosecutor, state senator, and founder of both the Natural Resources Defense Council and the South Street Seaport Museum. He passed away in 2019.

Ally Sheedy appeared in the films *The Breakfast Club*, *St. Elmo's Fire*, and *Only the Lonely*, and the critically acclaimed *High Art*. She has also published a collection of poetry entitled *Yesterday I Saw the Sun*.

Beverly Sills sang for many years with the Metropolitan Opera and the New York City Opera. She became chairwoman of the Lincoln Center for the Performing Arts and the Metropolitan Opera. She passed away in 2007.

Margaret Chase Smith represented the state of Maine as both a congresswoman and a senator. She was one of the first women to be nominated for presidency of the United States. She passed away in 1995.

Ronald B. Sobel is senior rabbi at the Temple Emanuel in New York City.

Stephen Sondheim, winner of both Tony and Academy Awards, wrote the lyrics for *West Side Story* and wrote both lyrics and music for *Company*, *Sunday in the Park with George*, *Into the Woods*, *Sweeney Todd*, and many others. He passed away in 2021.

Liv Ullmann, actress, author, and director, is honorary chair of the Women's Commission for Refugee Women and Children, vice-chairwoman of the International Rescue Committee, and a goodwill ambassador for UNICEF. She also participated in the 2010 Nobel Peace Prize Ceremony.

Kurt Vonnegut's novels include the classics *Cat's Cradle*, *The Sirens of Titan*, *Welcome to the Monkey House*, *Slaughterhouse Five*, *Galàpagos*, and *Bluebeard*. The American Humanist Association named him the Humanist of the Year in 1992. He passed away in 2007.

Wendy Wasserstein's plays include *Uncommon Women and Others*, *The Heidi Chronicles*, and *The Sisters Rosensweig*. She has won a Tony Award and a Pulitzer Prize for Drama. She passed away in 2006.

Paul Watkins is writer-in-residence at The Peddie School in New Jersey. His works include *Night over Day over Night*, *Stand before Your God*, *The Promise of Light*, and *The Ice Soldier*.

Elie Wiesel, winner of the Nobel Peace Prize, was the author of the *Night* trilogy. He passed away in 2016.

Elizabeth Winthrop, a writer for children and young adults, is the author of *The Castle in the Attic* and *The Battle for the Castle*.

Tom Wolfe, the author of *The Electric Kool-Aid Acid Test*, *The Right Stuff*, *Bonfire of the Vanities*, and *I Am Charlotte Simmons*, won the Academy of Achievement Golden Plate Award in 2005. He passed away in 2018.

Acknowledgments

Noel Coward, "I've Been to a Marvelous Party," copyright © 1945 by the Estate of Noel Coward. Reproduced by kind permission of Graham Payn, Esq.

Emily Dickinson, "Tell all the Truth But Tell It Slant," "If I can stop one Heart from breaking," and "I never saw a Moor." Reprinted by permission of the publishers and the Trustees of Amherst College from *The Poems of Emily Dickinson*, Thomas H. Johnson, ed., Cambridge, Mass.: The Belknap Press of Harvard University Press. Copyright © 1951, 1955, 1979, 1983, by the President and Fellows of Harvard College.

Excerpt from "Little Gidding" in *Four Quartets*, copyright © 1943 by T. S. Eliot and renewed 1971 by Esme Valerie Eliot. Reprinted by permission of Harcourt Brace & Company.

Robert Frost, "Stopping by Woods on a Snowy Evening" and "The Gift Outright," from *The Poetry of Robert Frost*, edited by Edward Connery Lathem. Copyright © 1942, 1951 by Robert Frost. Copyright © 1970 by Lesley Frost Ballantine. Copyright © 1923 by Henry Holt & Co., Inc. Reprinted by permission of Henry Holt & Co., Inc.

Langston Hughes, "Stars" and "To Be Somebody," from *Selected Poems* by Langston Hughes. Copyright © 1947, 1950 by Langston Hughes. Reprinted by permission of Alfred A. Knopf, Inc.